This book
belongs to:

....

....

Are You Shy?

Text: *Núria Roca*

Illustrations: *Marta Fàbrega*

BARRON'S

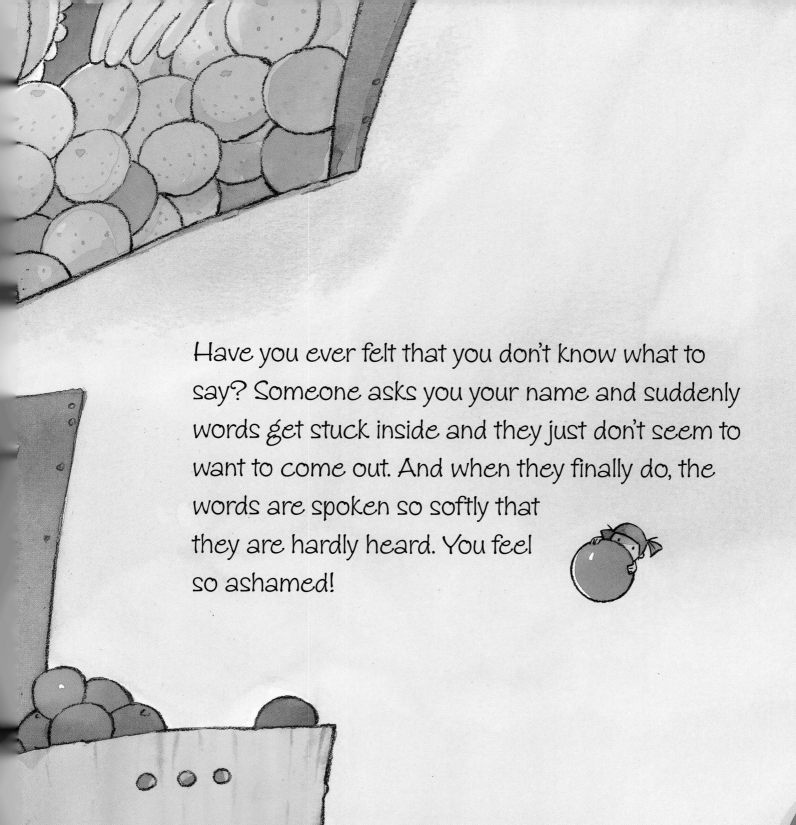

Have you ever felt that you don't know what to say? Someone asks you your name and suddenly words get stuck inside and they just don't seem to want to come out. And when they finally do, the words are spoken so softly that they are hardly heard. You feel so ashamed!

If you are a little shy, the best you can do is answer right away. There is no need to explain everything you did all day long! Sometimes, just by saying your name, you feel less shy and less ashamed.

There are boys and girls who are very, very shy. They are so shy that when they go to the park, they don't dare make new friends. They would love to jump and run and swing and...and play all kinds of other games with the rest of the kids! But they dare not ask if they would like to be friends. How would you go about making a new friend?

Sometimes making a new friend is a little hard. You watch him from a distance, you get closer, you keep watching him, you start playing nearby... By now, he certainly has noticed you! Now you can ask him if you can both play together. By playing with different kids you can get to know a lot of boys and girls and have a lot of fun with them!

Some shy kids think they do everything wrong. To them, everybody else is more fun, smarter, better-looking... more everything!

But actually, doing things well or badly is not that terribly important. What is important is that all of us have characteristics that make us special and unique... even when there are a few things we don't know how to do!

Mark is special because he knows so much about bats, Maria because she can ride a skateboard, Ralph because he helps with chores at home, and Paula—who is very shy—because she is learning to greet her parents' friends... How about you? Surely there are a lot of things that make you special!

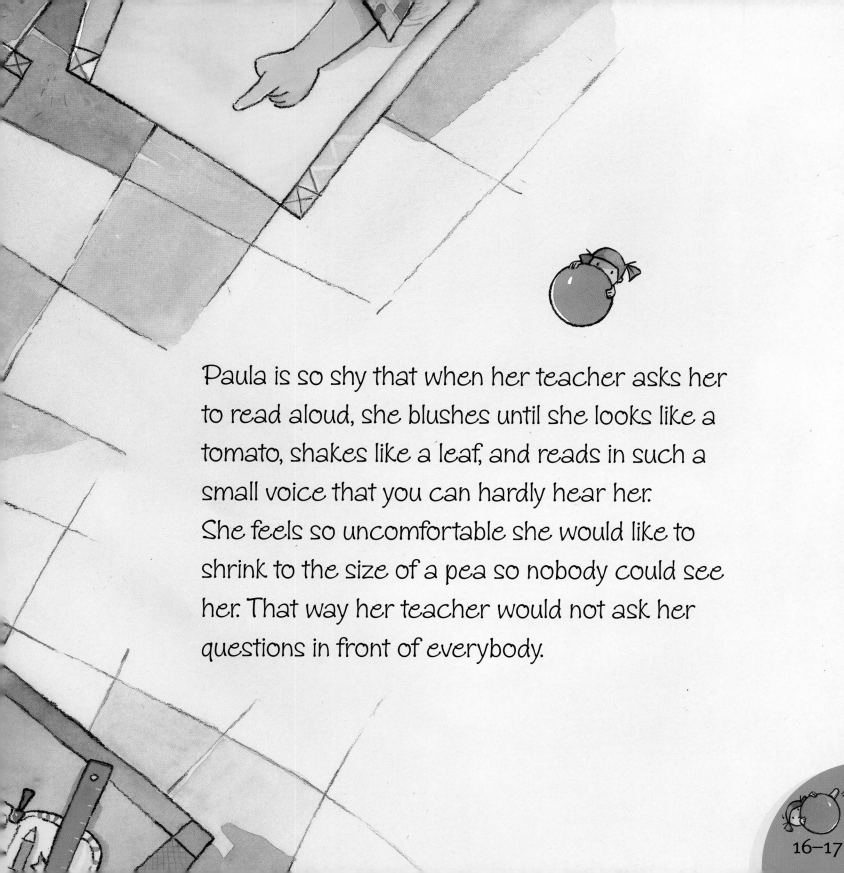

Paula is so shy that when her teacher asks her to read aloud, she blushes until she looks like a tomato, shakes like a leaf, and reads in such a small voice that you can hardly hear her. She feels so uncomfortable she would like to shrink to the size of a pea so nobody could see her. That way her teacher would not ask her questions in front of everybody.

Can you imagine how Paula must feel in front of a group of people she does not know? Her heart beats so fast it sounds like a runaway horse.

If this ever happens to you, try thinking about something you like very much or counting slowly up to three. One, two, three... One, two, three... One, two, three... Do you feel better now?

What Mark finds most difficult is saying no. That's why at lunchtime, he lets other kids take all his favorite snacks. He is afraid if he says no, his friends will leave him out. But if they were real friends, they would listen to Mark, wouldn't they? Is it hard for you to say no? If it is, you could practice in front of a mirror at home: no... no... NO!

I like... But I don't like... What do you like best in the world and what do you like least? And... do you dare tell people what you think or do you just let others decide for you?

It is all right to say how you feel and what you think about something, even if it is different from what others think. This way everybody will know you a little better and respect what you think and say.

Have you ever thought how a shy person must feel?
Close your eyes and imagine that in a show one of the
clowns decides to choose a kid from the audience to
be his helper. If the kid is shy... he might have a hard
time with this!
It would be better if the clown asked for a volunteer,
wouldn't it?

Nobody should laugh at a shy kid. And nobody should laugh at kids who wet their beds, or are afraid of balloons, or... can you think of any other examples? If you feel like laughing at somebody, think how this will hurt him or her. It's as if for just a moment, you became the other person. Can you imagine?

Sometimes shy people feel like hiding at home, as if they were a turtle in a shell. And turtles may be great, but we, unlike turtles, are capable of communicating and expressing our feelings unafraid. It doesn't matter if you

speak in a quiet voice or blush a deep red. The important thing is for you to talk. If you do, you will see that the feeling of embarrassment will disappear little by little.

guidelines
to parents

Being shy

Being shy is not the same as being an introvert. Shy kids relate to others less than they would like. They feel the drive to get close to other kids, but at the same time they avoid these situations. In this way, they are limiting their social contacts. If they just can't avoid certain situations, then they try to go unnoticed. Under these circumstances, it is best to avoid comments about your child's shyness when he or she is present—*"She's very shy," "He won't answer you," "She feels embarrassed,"*—and so on. Very often, shy people have low self-esteem. Making negative comments when they are speaking may cause them to pay more attention to what the other person might be thinking of them rather than to what they are trying to say.

What not to do

It is very important not to label your child as shy or to show irritation about this. Excess worry about their shyness or overprotecting them in social situations will make matters worse. Also, avoid the reproaches that make the child feel guilty, such as *"I suffer when you act like this,"* or *"You made me feel ashamed,"* or punishment by means of jokes or ironies (*"Cat got your tongue?"*). Such comments may increase the feelings of insecurity, so that a slight initial shyness may result in a crippling communication problem.

What to do

Show a tolerant and loving attitude, as well as understanding, so the child can feel sure of the love of grownups. As soon as possible, reinforce the child's social behavior and discuss any negative attitudes toward friends. Increase the child's self-esteem by encouraging his or her special abilities and provide activities in those areas, such as piano lessons, gymnastics, and so forth. So the children may learn to relate socially, it is important to put them in contact, little by little, with people of all ages.

A few suggestions

You may set some easy challenges for the child to increase her self-confidence: at a restaurant, ask him or her to order the food for the family with the help of a grownup; when shopping, allow her to have input about the clothes she would like to buy; when he gets dressed, let him decide among several options; sign her up for some group extracurricular activity that may help her socialize and increase her self-esteem (consider one in which she will feel comfortable: team sports, dancing, music, etc.).

At school

You may teach him strategies to reduce his anxiety. Consider teaching relaxation techniques, gradual exposure to the feared situation, practicing socializing at home with parental help as if it were a game, and so forth.

ARE YOU SHY?

Text: **Núria Roca**
Illustrations: **Marta Fàbrega**
Typesetting/design: **Gemser Publications, S.L.**

First edition for the United States and Canada published in 2006 by Barron's Educational Series, Inc.
Original title of the book in Spanish: *¿Hablas bajito?*
© Copyright 2006 by Gemser Publications, S.L.
El castell, 38; Teià (08329) Barcelona, Spain (World Rights)

All inquiries should be addressed to:
Barron's Educational Series, Inc.
250 Wireless Boulevard
Hauppauge, New York 11788
http://www.barronseduc.com

ISBN-13: 978-0-7641-3508-8
ISBN-10: 0-7641-3508-2
Library of Congress Control Number 2005938263

Printed in China
9 8 7 6 5 4 3 2 1